CULTURE CLASH

– RACISM

SCHOOL DAYS

The neighborhood I spent my childhood in was semi-rustic, middle-class, of standard L-shape three bedroom and two bath houses, with character as there was nothing of the tract housing placid monstrosity. The houses were individual and had largely fenced-in sides and backyards.

My father enjoyed gardening on his weekends. That was his pastime besides reading and then the holiday rise of holiday lights along the eaves. That task was always accomplished the weekend after Thanksgiving and then downed the weekend following New Year's.

Both my parents worked and were out of the house before dawn so I got myself up and to school in the morning. But usually my parents were home when I got home in the afternoon. It was a laborious prospect, as I didn't go to the public school nearby but miles away, and my commute involved a combination of walking and public transportation, in rain or shine. This was to ensure I had a private school education, as my mother valued private school as providing a superior education and less association with bad influences such as drugs.

The town I was raised in was largely crime-free, at least to the extent I didn't worry about crime and neither did my parents, with their children on their own so much.

I was only aware of a few of the neighbors on my block, none of whom had school-age children – girls – of my age. But the summer program at the public school often included a Parks & Rec person and – as kids - we enjoyed having something to do. There was also summer school if parents needed to park their kids somewhere for a few weeks. Want to learn how to build a birdhouse? Of course you do.

My parents' best friends were a Jewish and Catholic couple. They seemed to have an agreement to raise their children neutrally as they celebrated Christmas, but there was nothing overtly religious about it.

At my house, there was no conflict on religion and we celebrated Christmas but it didn't have religious overtones except for the obligatory manger set on a side table.

The children I was really familiar with came from all over the place, and some of them were through classes first through eight with me – grade school - and others came along for one year only or just a few. There was a high volume of military kids in the area, some of whom had parents stationed long-term or short-term.

There were biracial kids in school – Mexican and White as well as Black and

White ancestry – both in my class and also in other grades. It was nothing anyone blinked at.

My favorite teacher – of all time – was Black. I respected him and wanted his respect in return. He was the kind of teacher who seemed to understand each child independently of the whole, and brought out the best in us. He was great at teaching deportment and held himself with pride.

Much later I was asked about who my hero was and I said no one, but then I was insistently pressed about it and only one name came to mind, and it was this man.

I could also name my least favorite teacher of all time, and why. That name always came easily. A horrible woman – White - who can best be described as the woman on the bike trying to steal Toto from Dorothy. This terror proves parents' paying for a private school education takes too much for granted.

Asians were very common, one of whom was a friend of mine into high school years. I remember her father having a sharp sense of humor.   He drove us to movies and I could hang out at their house.

One of those kids who was in a grade with me for only one year was a girl – 'Marlene' - who was on the naughty side. Being a good kid, this was good exposure for me, something exciting and different. We became best friends quite separate from the clique that had been developed between me and closer friends of longer duration.

When I say 'Marlene' was on the naughty side, I mean we'd take off on our lunch break and go to a nearby store where she'd be busy packing away candy by virtue of dropping bars or packs into the vest over her blouse. In the meantime I'd be paying for mine at the register. It was exciting, that's what I got out of it. But eventually it was made clear the cashier knew what was going on and so we never went back. At least I don't remember going back with 'Marlene'. Remember, I wasn't stealing anything. But I'm sure I was too embarrassed to return.

By the way, 'Marlene' was biracial, half Black, half White. I never asked her about it, because I didn't need to. It wasn't a thing. The giveaway was the hair and skin color. Though I learned later on that biracial kids usually had difficulties, which was not in our community.

There must have been something in my character as I entered high school without any firm friends in place, but fell into an even bigger clique that cushioned me, especially since a new best friend – 'Suzie' – was of Mexican ancestry and also on the naughty side. How naughty? Well, when I met her she already had one pregnancy behind her. And she loved shoplifting. Again, shoplifting. Maybe this is what girls do for kicks? I was bemused, for the most part, enjoying the thrill of being on the inside. It doesn't take much to thrill a kid, and I wasn't into smoking or drugs, and maybe – as a perfect child – this was my form of rebellion. I have no idea what happened to 'Suzie' as we lost contact when she graduated from high school. She was a year ahead of me. And pregnant again. I like to think I learned from observation and repeating others' mistakes wasn't for me. I didn't want a police record or an unwanted pregnancy. Or worse, being a single mom with no regular income.

There was 'Laura' whom I knew from grade school, and I went to her house which was in an exclusive community – I understood now the difference between middle-class (where I was) and upper-middle-class (where she was). 'Laura's' personal issue was feeling the sting and burden of being an only child. Nowadays we'd call her a token. Her parents – she felt – had high expectations for her she wouldn't be able to fulfill. Her mother was a doctor and her father held elected office.

'Laura' was not bi-racial, as both her parents were Black.

Later, there was a TV show about the Huxtable family and I thought about 'Laura' and wondered at the big deal. From what I knew, Blacks could be upper class.

My friend – 'Cindy' – was of Asian ancestry, and she was a sweet, uncomplicated, never-in-trouble girl who had one bad thing going for her, as far as I was concerned, and that was her extremely long ratty black hair. I had no idea why it was never cut. I thought the weight of it should cause her headaches and didn't look attractive.   At least even out the ends, I thought.

The only physical altercation I ever witnessed between girls was in high school and was a knock-down, drag-out-pulling off the earring between a Black and a Hispanic girl, neither of whom I knew personally or had any idea of what their disagreement was about. I was stunned at the ferocity and amazed anyone would get into a physical altercation over anything. Let alone in the middle of the school grounds. And the thought of the bleeding ear just bothered me. I think it delayed me getting my ears pierced for just that reason.

A teacher in our senior year of high school - who was from out-of-state - mentioned all us students were off in a cloud and we'd be given a shock when we entered the real world. The discussion was racism, and everyone in this school – at least in this class - figured racism had been settled by the Civil War.

I guess I was still in a cloud over what she said, for a few more years.

YOUNG ADULT

I was working a temporary assignment for a government office in Arizona and I was there for about two weeks when I suddenly lifted my head from my task of filing – barely listening to the discussion going on around me – when I realized out of the half-dozen women occupying desks and the other people in the room, I was the only White person. It was secretly amusing to me; it had taken me that long to pick up on this.

When I mentioned this to my mother she told me a lot of minorities find government jobs their best security.

Was this when I first felt an outsider? Not really. I had been gradually aware my lack of language skills – especially not knowing Spanish – was debilitating to me and my future. I wanted to know what people were saying around me, wanting to be inclusive and not exclusive, someone apart.

By this time I had traveled a bit and seen apparently all-White communities, and that's the sole reason they stood out to me. There was a gated community I visited where a restaurant was a good stop for a coffee break and one day what caught my attention was four Black women and one White woman at the same table, in discussion over something. The Black women grouping together I now knew was typical but I kept wondering how the White woman figured into it.

But this temporary clerk job made me aware there was a difference between me and other people. Though there was nothing overtly negative towards me – as a White person – from the Hispanic and Blacks who were in the room.

I think I didn't exist. But I wondered if these women accepting each other as co-workers, did they ghost me not because I was a Temp but because I was White? I thought it more likely it was because I was a Temp. Temp workers are rarely worth getting to know. They are here today and gone tomorrow, that's their function. So there was no purpose in getting to know me. But that was years ago, and now I reflect on it and wonder.

In my social life, worse were the children of the super-wealthy who were lightly dismissive of me due to my class and not because I was White, because they were too. Someone I was friendly with on a daily basis hadn't invited me to a party at his house, and then I knew where I stood. It was ostracism due to my being lower class. Since I was comfortable with middle and upper class due my own upbringing – and having had friends in both environments – it was odd for me to adjust to be something OTHER. But the shut-out had to do with economics and not race.

I started paying attention to who paid attention to whom and why. Life was more complicated than I knew and that

teacher from high school was right
about that.

SERIOUS BUSINESS

At a certain point you have to think about the future. Long-term, post-working-age, retirement future. And a friend recommended I join a big firm that offered health and retirement benefits. If I could survive that long, that is. This meant a Union job and having no experience with Unions before, I learned the history and how important they are to advance any economic justice.

Here, I became a big fan of unions in general, but learned they were not perfect. I saw too many employees who would have been fired in a normal (non-union) job keep hanging on, due to Union influence. And I felt affronted by that. The bad ones should go, I thought. But it didn't matter the color of the person, it had to do with their work ethic.

Again, this was a huge company surrounded by Whites and a variety of Asian cultures, Hispanics, Blacks, you name it. The difference was only in the job title, which detailed your status and income.

But it was a huge operation.

Once a Black man who was in line in front of me at the company cafeteria was boasting to me in high energy about how he was assigned his own clerk, and he'd never had that before. He was so thrilled - while he was waiting on his food order - and I was just behind him, with no one else in line. I think he was trying to impress me, taking me for management, because once I told him my job title, he shut down fast. I got back at him when his plate was delivered to me and I noted "That's a lot of cholesterol." It was.

I worked with a lot of Blacks and I noted something I hadn't been in a position to notice before, and that's the cultural difference between us. For someone Black, if there was a discussion of a famous Black man or woman they would discuss that person on a first-name basis, as if that notable was their cousin or brother or sister or something. As a White person, we tend to refer to the famous in full-name terms, we are not that familiar with them, never refer to them as if we are familial.

I realized Blacks were watching different TV shows and movies than me. They went to Baptist Churches as if anything else would be revolutionary, and even behaved as if the Church was an extension of their own family. One person, she was part of a congregation headed by her uncle and only family members were in that congregation. Did that even count?

Blacks drove white cars or black cars or name-your-shade of beige cars. And their houses were bland as well, the décor in off-white and white and name-your-shade of beige.

The clothing was dark, tans, browns, black and white. I wondered why there wasn't more color in their world. Of course there was animal prints - lots of animal prints - and I guessed a homage to the continent of Africa.

My world had so much color in comparison.

But why didn't they see their skin tone was more flattered by yellows and greens, etc.? When a woman of color shows up on TV I silently cheer if she is wearing a color that is flattering to her.

And I respected recycling efforts and noted my work group had several Blacks in it and none of them recycled at all. They said it was too much trouble.

I also became close friends with a Filipino lady and we spent a lot of breaks together. When she retired I was the only non-Filipino at her retirement celebration. I felt bad because they were all speaking English – instead of Tagalog – only because I was at the table. I hated inhibiting people like this.

Otherwise I noticed my small clique was comprised of all White people.

I remained close with one of my Black friends who had left the company, seeking better pastures for a rise in her career prospects. We socialized by shopping and going to movies together and I knew her husband and children. I wasn't her only White friend, either, and she and her husband had a wide experience of the country, being a former military family. It came to me military families probably are more invisible to color and more tolerable of scant differences. I can say Church never came up at all.

Blacks tend not to tip. When wait staff deserves a tip, tip properly, that's how I was raised. The tip is the majority of their income. But Blacks tend not to tip and don't feel aggrieved about it. I wondered if the wait staff at these restaurants secretly cursed or groaned whenever a Black person was having a sit-down meal.

As time went on I acquired another close Black friend. There were occasional issues between me and her. Let's call her 'Linda'. She was a great one for calling the RACE CARD whenever it suited her, like it was a mantra she'd pull out without clear thought. One time I told her there were buses of Asians who would come into the state to do shopping tours, then there were also the Asian bus tours that were about buying real estate. Immediately 'Linda' was crying foul! Or "That's racist." I corrected her that when you are stating a fact – as there were shopping tours for both shopping and real estate purchases – that was not racist. The Brits who were taking flights to visit the Mall of America, was that racist to point that out? 'Linda' tried to pass it off as if it hadn't happened, whenever she was stumped.

I learned 'Linda's' history included calling NAACP to register complaints whenever she was expected to perform the same workload as any of her co-workers in the same job. But she wasn't the only one to pull the NAACP complaint card.

'Linda' didn't work very much. She would get on committees so she could spend time in a meeting or take on a function that took about five minutes of work but claim it took two or more hours.

'Linda' often tried to corral me and others into doing her work or would pass off anything she didn't want to do, like transferring calls to co-workers without any intro, just a call dump. She either didn't know how to fix the problem or didn't want to handle the workload. She didn't have the best expertise in the job, as if she was averse to learning. But 'Linda's' phone number would show up on the display on our phones and when I told her I didn't appreciate her transferring work to me like that she would say she hadn't, but eventually she stopped doing it.

She also did her son's homework a lot: tried to get me to do it too.

There was a friend of 'Linda's' who worked the Union and therefore the system, and arranged nervous breakdowns when she didn't get the vacation time she wanted, that sort of thing. It finally got to the point no one wanted her around anymore, not even other Blacks. There are people who are working hard, and people like this made them look bad.   And made them angry.

My other friends – outside the work place - were White. I say this had more to do with the activities involved. It was about attending concerts and the theater and traveling to sci-fi conventions and traveling in general. At this point I was sitting in audiences and scanning the audience and realizing it was all White people. So that meant there were audiences out there comprised of solely Black people. It seemed odd, like something was happening I wasn't aware of. But it had to do with society and we were two societies now.

But not everyone in my orbit was White. A close friend for many years was Asian-American but we shared the same interests and we had a great time together until my rising fortunes and her falling ones drew us apart.

MOWING THE WEEDS

With my first house a friend of mine told me "You just moved to Mexico." Huh? I didn't know what she meant except a neighbor to one side of me was blaring Mexican music full blast – as in you could hear it throughout the block. The other side neighbor, no problem at all.

But there was the neighbor two doors down, he was Mexican ancestry, who was somewhat obtuse to my rejection of his attempted affection. I was opening up my garage door one morning and there was a weird thumping going on, it turned out his daughter had ridden her bike up onto my driveway and left it leaning against my garage door.   I left it out in the curb and my view from a window showed a puzzled looking would-be suitor retrieving it.

My full-blast music neighbors turned out to be funneling illegal Mexicans, the kind who hang out in front of one of those contractor stores in hopes of getting hired for the day. Now I feel sorry for those guys, often taken advantage of, sometimes they do the work then get stiffed the pay. Their occupancy was apparently cots in the garage. The driveway and in front of the house had the giveaway of too many people with the amount of cars crowding the area.

This is when I found out this city of 100,000 and more had literally no sound/noise ordinances at all. So these guys had a right to be talking loudly throughout the night on their driveway, and you know how sound carries at night, especially when it's otherwise silent. Remember how people are supposed to hear crickets, and that's when you know you're in a good place?

But it wasn't just them. The man across the street – he was White – was working on his vehicle in the garage until early morning, at least 2am. Why? Probably to get away from his family.

That's what man-caves – and garages – are for.

The trespassing – and tossing of trash into my yard – was so bad I took pains to have a tall fence enclosure built. Turns out there was still trespassing – my driveway seemed to be the thoroughfare for pick-ups and drop-offs.

As well, when I got the gutters checked out, it revealed items like shampoo bottles.

A police officer came out for a consult with me, that's when I found out about there being no noise restrictions. But he told me there were all sorts of other restrictions that were on board for trouble spots like this. What restrictions? No drinking alcohol in driveways, parking violations aplenty. They could probably find others as well.

I didn't even tell the policeman about the illegals in the garage. I always had sympathy for them as they have a rough time of it.

But I had a name and number to call if I wanted to pursue these objectives.

By the way, the apartment complex to the rear of me was a place for drug deals and often police were cruising the area, sometimes with a kid shouting a warning to some older guy that was doing business against a building. How do I know this? Because I had a dog to walk, my first house and my first dog, and I was diligent about my dog walking responsibility.

There was even an occasion where more than a dozen vehicles were surrounding an apartment complex while helicopters were overheard, obviously having cornered somebody.

What was revealed during these walks was how this neighborhood was now a mixed-bag of lower class and slum combined with hanging-in-there upper middle class or middle class. This was revealed by clean properties devoid of multi-cars and obviously major expenses put into landscaping and maintenance. Also very little tract housing except on my mixed-bag street.

Some of these houses I wondered if the residents were reluctant to move despite what was happening to the neighborhood around them. Usually, if your own block is secure and comfortable, you have no reason to move. Problems within your block – I've since learned - are enough to cause agitation and distress, usually resulting in the good neighbor selling up.

My neighborhood wasn't a good neighborhood but oddly it was getting better – for me – when my bad neighbors next door moved on. And – FUNNY! – they moved into a town that was so restricted in the behavior of its residents the entire town functioned as a non-gated HOA. The entire town! I knew this because a friend of mine lived there.

She even told me about how some of the residents took up the task themselves to cruise the neighborhoods, taking photographs and making detailed notes to pass on to the local police – not that the police were happy about that. I'm certain my former neighbors just believed they were moving up in the world and could still get away with whatever they wanted to, but unfortunately – for them – they must have gotten quite a kick in the pants, because violations meant a totaling up of heavy fines.

I wasn't settled into my forever home, yet. A lot of us have a first home and then move up.

So I moved to a largely rural community. It was a risk but I never seemed risk averse.

So in my restless search for the perfect retirement community, I ventured into extremes.

My neighbors – largely White, Republican and Church-going – were cold and remote, no welcome-to-the-neighborhood that didn't involve some invitation to join their Church.

The word was out the surrounding coldness was "All the Californians." I was skeptical because I knew native Southern Californians who moved to this state but into a Metro zone. They lasted less than a year, complaining about their unfriendly neighbors.

Through time, meeting one person or another – always briefly – they might know or knew someone who knows someone in my neighborhood. And my neighborhood contained people from Idaho, Montana, and even New York. I wondered why everyone wanted to blame California.

One woman who was from California always said she "hated California." Finally I asked her why and she stumbled over it then said "It's too crowded." Then I knew she was drawn

here, if not for smaller population,
maybe the 99% White population.

Of course if you belonged to a Church,
or the extremely vocal Republican
Party, that meant you weren't excluded,
you were now a member of the family.
But if you refused to join a collective,
that let you be easily ostracized.

I only ever saw one Black man in town,
and he worked at the big mart. It was
an all-purpose store, but nothing quaint
about it. At customer service or at the
checkout, this attractive man in his
thirties seemed efficient and good at
his job.

This shopping center was so large,
when working off a shopping list – no
matter how many times I'd been to this
store – I was having to read the signs
over the aisles to check if I needed to
venture down that one. I hated wasting
time looking for stuff.

This one time I was about to push my
cart into the aisle when a woman was

coming toward me. She was Black – the only Black woman I'd seen in years, at this point – and her cart and mine might have collided. But she halted at my confusion. I instantly hoped she didn't get the wrong impression. My eyes falling down her body had to do with how smartly she was dressed. Like on the cover of a magazine. In this area the wealthy dressed like hobos. And I still didn't know if I needed any item down that aisle. So I raised my eyes to read the overhead banner and there was nothing there that had to do with my list. As she was waiting on me to make my decision I pulled my cart away from its half-circle and moved to the next aisle.

Did she think I was trying to avoid a person of color?

I was really wanting to compliment her on her style but to do so would point out she was overdressed for the area.

Did she realize I was a confused shopper?

Was she the sister or wife of the man who worked here?

Whatever was happening in her mind, I never saw her again, and not too long afterwards I realized the store clerk was gone too.

Why is this chapter calling Mowing the Weeds? Because that's what you did here, as with frequent rain there are frequent weeds. So you'd better be equipped with an edger and mow the weeds as if you're mowing the lawn.

MOVING ON (in years)

As if that wasn't enough, I deliberately moved back into the real world, as I saw it. I moved into a city where Whites ruled all the top offices in the County yet Whites were the clear minority in the population.

There was a young woman I first took exception to. She was Black and I saw her cross a street to a house I knew wasn't hers and she went and sat on a chair on that property. She was using her cell phone. I was inclined to dislike her. But one day we passed time together, had one of those instantly connecting conversations, and I put to the back of my mind the image of her occupying someone else's property. We saw each other quite frequently, as if instant long-term friends. Then as things go, many months passed before we ran into each other in a store. She was calling out to me, which got my attention and then I was so pleased to see her I almost gave her a hug, but I reminded myself we weren't that close - I had even deleted her entry in my Contact List.

Unfortunately, in my new house and property, I felt like I was being terrorized. I had never experienced before children – and their parents – who disregarded all decorum. As far as the parents were concerned, as they stated, "You are the problem." Me, because I complained about them, their constant intrusions into my property, their children tossing trash into my yard and tormenting my dogs. Not to mention all the noise, of their private cell phone conversations that blared through my house, at all hours.

And it wasn't just me, I eventually learned. Once they knew what house I was in, I was collecting complaints from other neighbors about my neighbors.

The police were of no assistance. "We don't do houses." That's what they said.

I complained frequently to the owner-landlord of that house. But the monthly check-in-the-mail secured landlord's complicity.

Another neighbor - an elderly White woman - volunteered to do yard cleanup for her Black neighbor because otherwise it wouldn't get done.

Walking the neighborhood, it seems the cleanliness of the yard is part of the rental agreements – or County Code - no one Black seems to care about.

And the streets in front of the houses are plagued with broken glass and toys and trash.

I've noticed Blacks walking right past litter on their property – or contributing to it! – as if it's invisible. Or picking up the trash and throwing it into other neighbors' yards.

Most of the Blacks who have dogs have large breeds that never leave the backyard. I hear them barking day and night. They are only kept for that purpose, I guess. Those poor dogs.

Someone I know told me his family lives in a gated community only because when there are problems with renters or homeowners it was dealt with. Tenants evicted, owners changing their ways or selling. Either way, problem solved via the HOA.

There are a variety of problems. This means many of the long-term neighbors were and are selling up. Some of these houses have been pocketed by the government for low-rent assistance – the local and dreaded Section 8 - or investors who want properties to lease, safely in a neighborhood in which they don't live.

But it's not only Blacks moving in, but it seems Whites are the ones moving out.

It's usually Whites complaining about loud music and other offenses, but it's also some Hispanics, who yearn to complain about their neighbors but

fear any pay-back visit from
Immigration.

I know not every Hispanic is into racing
a horse until it collapses in death or
cock fights or dog fights, but many are.

In any neighborhood there needs to be
a complicit – yet silent – agreement
that all the residents observe a certain
code of acceptable behavior just as we
all have to follow certain laws. But this
isn't being done as more and more
neighbors turn a blind eye to the
unspoken rules.

Take a drive through any neighborhood
on the fringe and you will quickly spot
the ugly house, the eyesore which is as
jarring as touring a new auto
dealership showroom only to be
suddenly confronted with a wreck.

The step-up for new residents is turned
into a step-down – or step away – for
others. Because of neighbors who don't
fulfil the bargain they signed onto when

they moved into that good
neighborhood.

So when I see a Black child, I wince.

And when I see a Black teenager, I
wonder which direction he/she is going
to turn.

When I see a Black adult, of either sex, I
wonder if they raise their kids with foul
language and abhorrent behavior and
how this appears to be the future.

I want to tell them, just because you
spit out the seeds that doesn't finish
your job at parenting.

I know raising your children
surrounded with language like
"motherfucking" every other word is
because of HIP HOP as multi-
generations listen to the music and
hear the language and shrug it off.

I do as well.

And it must be hard to tell a child not to
use that language when a parent is

using it so casually, sometimes more than once in a sentence.

The truth is, before this I had never had a Black neighbor before, merely by coincidence, not design. But now I wonder if with all of my prior associations, was their behavior an exception or would I have found those friendships in danger if I had lived next door to them, if we were in the same neighborhood, would there have been conflicts? One made of different social standards.

It could be we are just not compatible.

I've come to the same conclusion that I believe many White (human rights) activists have, that Black Lives Matter as long as they're somewhere else.